MINISTERING IN A CHANGING SEXUAL LANDSCAPE

A GUIDE TO HELPING
THOSE WITH
SEXUAL ISSUES

Edward E. Moody, Jr., Ph.D.

114 Bush Rd I Nashville, TN 37217
randallhouse.com

© 2015 by Edward E. Moody

Published by Randall House Publications
114 Bush Road
Nashville, TN 37217

All rights reserved. No part of this publication may be reproduced, stored in a retrieval system, or transmitted in any form or by any means—electronic, mechanical, photocopy, recording, or any other means—except for brief quotation in critical reviews, without the prior permission of the publisher.

All Scripture quotations are from The Holy Bible, English Standard Version® (ESV®) Copyright © 2001 by Crossway, a publishing ministry of Good News Publishers. All rights reserved.

Printed in the United States of America

ISBN-13: 978-0-89265-986-9

> Jesus Christ is the same yesterday and today and forever.
> **HEBREWS 13:8**

God does not change, but the world is changing the way it views sexual issues at a rapid pace. Politicians are "evolving" in their views about the definition of marriage. Churches are shifting away from what has been taught for millennia apparently influenced by the world. If you believe in a biblical view of sexuality you may find yourself increasingly out of step with the world around you.

We must effectively deal with this changing climate. It is the issue of our time. We can look back in history to see the impact of volatile issues. What became known as the Scopes Monkey Trial was held in Dayton, Tennessee in 1925, William Jennings Bryan defended the biblical teaching, that God created the world as John T. Scopes was prosecuted for teaching evolution in a Tennessee public school. Though Christians appeared to have won in the courtroom (Scopes was convicted, yet the conviction was later overturned on a technicality), Christians suffered defeat in the court of public opinion. At the time, the majority of Americans (many still do) agreed with the Christian teaching on the origin of the world, but after the event many Christians began to retreat from the public square (e.g., the media, the arts, and higher education).[1]

As a result, you might hear someone who does not subscribe to the theory of evolution called a "flat earther," and see presidential candidates that express doubt about the theory ridiculed. The biblical teaching on the creation of the world is less and less part of the mainstream. Will history repeat itself? To date, most Christians have used the polls and courts to push back against sexual sin in the U.S. For many years it appeared that Christians were winning at the polls and in the courts. However, as Putnam and Campbell noted, Christians appear to have won arguments in the political arena while losing the cultural war by fighting too hard.[2] Perhaps many of these efforts were misplaced. As James Hunter has noted, political action does not usually lead to cultural change.[3] We need to understand our current landscape if we hope to influence it.

> *Behold, I am sending you out as sheep in the midst of wolves, so be wise as serpents and innocent as doves.*
>
> MATTHEW 10:16

THE NEW LANDSCAPE

While Christians were focused on the courts and the polls, the cultural heart of America shifted and many now view Christians negatively. It helps to assess what has happened. Timothy Keller summarized H. Richard Niebuhr's cycle of the church's relationship to culture into four seasons.[4]

In the winter, the church is in a hostile relationship with a pre-Christian culture and is gaining little traction. There is little distinctive, vital Christian life and community with no evangelistic fruit. In the spring, the Church is embattled, even persecuted by a pre-Christian culture, but it is growing. China is an example of this season. In the summer, the culture is allied with the church. The church is highly regarded by the public and there will be many Christians in the centers of cultural production. Christians feel at home in the culture. This describes America and much of the West previously. In the autumn, Christians are marginalized in this culture. Christian ideals may be viewed as antiquated and out of step with this culture. This is where we find much of the West today. This slide into autumn can be different depending upon where you minister, but it is important to realize autumn is here or rapidly approaching and you must prepare to minister in the different landscape.[5]

You may not feel that the community you are in is in a cultural autumn. Different parts of the United States are in different seasons as can be seen by religious participation. The Deep South, Mississippi valley, and Utah are the most religious areas of the country, while the northeast and western United States are the least. Regardless of where you live, the influence of Christianity upon young adults is waning. The number of young adults (ages 18-29) who mark "no religious preference" on surveys has risen to 20 percent,[6] and many have an increasingly negative view of biblical Christianity. Eighty-five percent say that Christians are hypocritical, and 87 percent view Christians as judgmental.[7]

The result can be seen in the rejection of Christian teachings on sexuality and marriage. Today 7 in 10 of 18-33 year-olds support same-sex marriage.[8] Traditional Christianity is being rejected, and instead of seeing Christians and Christianity as a source of hope for homosexuals, 91 percent of those in studies view Christians as anti-homosexual and only 23 percent see Christianity as a source of hope.[9] It is becoming increasingly difficult to minister to those around us. Perhaps the situation is the most difficult at any point in the history of the United States. What are we to do? Let us not retreat like many Christians did after Scopes in 1925. Let us consider some fellow believers from the past who have faced similar if not more difficult challenges than we. What can we learn from them?

THE RIGHT MODEL

For whatever was written in former days was written for our instruction, that through endurance and through the encouragement of the Scriptures we might have hope.

ROMANS 15:4

LOT THE PROSPERER

We can find hope today when we look to the patriarch's of the past. If we think we have problems let us consider Lot. Though a brother in the faith, Lot shows us what not to do. We meet Lot in the Bible as he leaves Ur with Abram (Genesis 11:31). The author notes (Genesis 13:5), he had flocks, herds, and tents. You might say he had the house, a minivan, the good job, and a couple of kids. He was doing pretty well for himself. Next, we see conflict between those who worked for Abram and those who worked for Lot. Abram suggested they separate. The Scripture says that Lot saw "that the Jordan Valley was well watered everywhere" (Genesis 13:10). Lot was looking

---

Are you motivated by money or meaning?

Results of the Faith Matters Survey (2006) indicated that secular Americans view highly religious Americans as selfish.[10]

For where your treasure is, there your heart will be also.
MATTHEW 6:21

for and may have embraced the new landscape of Sodom because of what it seemed to offer. Early on in the Bible there are hints that prosperity and luxury are more important to Lot than the safety of being with God's people, "while Lot settled among the cities of the valley and moved his tent as far as Sodom. Now the men of Sodom were wicked, great sinners against the LORD" (Genesis 13:12b–13). It seems Lot was more interested in upward mobility than establishing a strong spiritual foundation for his family. Interestingly, many nonbelievers today claim that Christians are more concerned with making money and being a success than living a meaningful life.

Asleep at the Wheel

Though prosperous, Sodom was a dangerous place. In a frightening turn of events, Lot was kidnapped. Abraham rescued Lot (Genesis 14). Still Lot stayed in Sodom, perhaps wanting his family to have the best clothes and amenities that money could buy, which were not available outside of Sodom. We know that Sodom was a very prosperous place and Lot prospered there, as he seemed to be a leader. In those days, someone who sat at the gate of a city as Lot did (Genesis

> Behold, this was the guilt of your sister Sodom: she and her daughters had pride, <u>excess of food, and prosperous ease</u>, but did not aid the poor and needy.
> Ezekiel 16:49

> **Not a D6 Family**
> *Hear, O Israel: The Lord our God, the Lord is one. You shall love the Lord your God with all your heart and with all your soul and with all your might. And these words that I command you today shall be on your heart. You shall teach them diligently to your children, and shall talk of them when you sit in your house, and when you walk by the way, and when you lie down, and when you rise. You shall bind them as a sign on your hand, and they shall be as frontlets between your eyes. You shall write them on the doorposts of your house and on your gates.*
> Deuteronomy 6:4–9

19:1) was a person of renown. Lot was a success. Later, the men of Sodom would seem to be resentful of him as they said, "This fellow came to sojourn, and he has become the judge!" (Genesis 19:9). Though Lot was a success in Sodom, it does not appear he was very successful as a husband or father or at influencing those around him toward the Lord. Perhaps the demands he faced to maintain his position allowed little time to try to influence others.

Lot was not a *D6 Father*. Though he lived in a time before the book of Deuteronomy had been given, he did not take advantage of the truth he had. It is unlikely that he spent a lot of time teaching the truth about God and how to interact with the community. Lot's prosperity ended in failure.

God decided to destroy Sodom. When the moment

of truth came and Lot tried to influence his sons-in-law to leave the city, he seemed to them to be "jesting" (Genesis 19:14). As the destruction of the city was about to begin he "lingered" (Genesis 19:16). Even after Sodom was destroyed, he begged to be allowed to live near a city (Genesis 19:20). His own wife longingly looked back and was destroyed just like Sodom (Genesis 19:26). Then after Lot and his daughters escaped to a cave, they got him intoxicated and each became intimate with him (Genesis 19:30–38).

> *And if he rescued righteous Lot, greatly*
> *distressed by the sensual conduct of the wicked.*
>
> 2 Peter 2:7

What can we learn from Lot?

> *Keep your conduct among the Gentiles honorable, so that when they speak against you as evildoers, they may see your good deeds and glorify God on the day of visitation.*
>
> 1 Peter 2:12

Lot was a lot like many today that have as their main goal the prosperity and popularity of their family. As they chase after their goals, they may not have time for God's people (those in their extended family and the church). Lot was like many who are too busy with leisure activities or sports or dance or this or that, which robs them of the time they should be spending building their

> *And let us consider how to stir up one another to love and good works, not neglecting to meet together, as is the habit of some, but encouraging one another, and all the more as you see the Day drawing near.*
> Hebrews 10:24–25

family, and fellowshipping around God's Word at a local church. Christian families are very busy today, just not on the things that matter the most. Too many do not take the time to influence those around them toward the Lord. Lot's family, though important, and apparently influential, had little spiritual impact upon the culture they adopted. When real trouble arose and Lot tried to save his family, his sons-in-law did not listen, his wife looked back, and Lot's daughters took indecent liberties with him—not seeing how bad it was to violate God's standards for holiness. The Bible tells us in 2 Peter 2:7 that "righteous Lot" was "greatly distressed by the sensual conduct of the wicked" in Sodom. He was bothered by it, but ineffective in doing anything about it.

From Lot we learn that accommodation of the culture does not work. In the end, you do not change the culture, but one day you wake up and realize the culture has changed you and your family in the areas of life that really matter.

> *You are the salt of the earth, but if salt has lost its taste, how shall its saltiness be restored? It is no longer good for anything except to be thrown out and trampled under people's feet.*
> Matthew 5:13

Be Salt and Light to Your Community

Lot failed to be salt and light to Sodom. Though everyone appeared to have known him, he did not appear to have a spiritual influence upon Sodom. Why? Similarly, today 84 percent of young people say they know at least one committed Christian. Lot's problem may be found in what people say about Christians today. Only 15 percent say the lifestyles of Christians are different from their own.[12]

> Among young people who are not Christians, 84 percent report knowing at least one committed Christian. Only 15 percent report that the lifestyles of Christians are different from their own.[11]

Today in increasing numbers in the United States, nonbelievers point out the hypocrisy of Christians saying they watch the same movies, listen to the same music, and engage in the same behaviors. In fact, Christian's divorce, engage in sexual promiscuity, and view pornography just like nonbelievers. In surveys comparing Christians to non-Christians, there is little statistical difference. The findings are worse when you look at young adults as a generation seems to be sliding away from biblical Christianity nonbelievers ask, "Where is the difference?" This results in devastating consequences for Christians as well as the world around them.

Where's the Difference?[13]
What have you done in the last 30 days?

	Christians	Non-Christians
Viewed Pornography	30%	35%
Used Profanity in Public	26%	38%
Bought a Lottery Ticket	26%	34%

Recently a study was published in the American Journal of Sociology entitled "Red states, blue states and divorce: Understanding the impact of conservative Protestantism on regional variations of divorce rates."[15] The researchers examined demographic data of all 50 states. They found that the proportion of conservative Protestants in a county was positively correlated to divorce. In other words, your risk for divorce is higher when there are more people who proclaim to be Christians in the community. Unfortunately, this is likely to lead many to claim that Christianity is bad for marriage. We know this is not the case, and other research supports this. For example, Wilcox's work,

Slip Sliding Away[14]
Activities young Christians report engaging in during the last 30 days

Viewed sexually explicit content	36%
Sex outside of marriage	18%
Gotten drunk	24%
Bought a Lottery ticket	25%
Used profanity in public	36%
Said mean things about others	36%

Soft Patriarchs, New Men: How Christianity Shapes Fathers and Husbands indicates that families actively participating in conservative Christian churches actually fair much better than other groups on a plethora of measures.[16] However, what this data does show is that there are many "Lot's" in our community today and the way they are living their lives is having detrimental effects upon themselves and those around them. Many are what the book of Revelation refers to as lukewarm. They pay little attention to following the Lord and it results in major family problems. Further, at best, they are ineffective in helping the families around them. It is critical that we learn from Lot's misfortune the importance of living a godly life because when Lot speaks, the world laughs, and the result is destruction.

> *I know your works: you are neither cold nor hot. Would that you were either cold or hot! So, because you are lukewarm, and neither hot nor cold, I will spit you out of my mouth.*
> Revelation 3:15–16

Train Your Children

What happened to Lot's children? We know at least up until the destruction of Sodom they had remained sexually pure (Genesis 19:8). Yet, after the destruction of Sodom they did the unthinkable with their father (Genesis 19:30–38). The actions of Lot, offering them to the Sodomites (Genesis 19:8), may have terribly impacted them. The culture of Sodom combined with a loss of respect for their father, may have influenced their horrific act of incest with their father. Similarly, the culture around our youth combined with the behavior of parents may have negatively impacted youth in America. What is the impact of a culture, combined with the knowledge of a parent's pornography use or extramarital affair upon a young person? Perhaps our plight is not unlike that of Lot's family.

Many are quick to claim that the behavior of a family has no impact upon the well being of the family. Further, many claim there is no impact upon a family that is constituted contrary to the design in Scripture. To support these claims much research has been cited that has examined the opinion of parents on the well-being of their children. Recently, sociologist Mark Regnerus conducted a study where instead of surveying parents he examined the actual children of those who had grown up in families impacted by divorce, cohabitation, and with same-sex parents. He found that the children in what might be defined as more traditional families (as described in Scripture) reported fairing better than the other family constellations.[17]

Go on offense by building a strong family. Lot could have helped Sodom, and we can help our communities by building strong families that invest in our community. That is what Jeremiah instructed Judah to do as they went into Babylon as exiles.

> *Build houses and live in them; plant gardens and eat their produce. Take wives and have sons and daughters; take wives for your sons, and give your daughters in marriage, that they may bear sons and daughters; multiply there, and do not decrease. But seek the welfare of the city where I have sent you into exile, and pray to the Lord on its behalf, for in its welfare you will find your welfare.*
>
> JEREMIAH 29:5–7

Instead of hiding from the world, Jeremiah told the exiles to live, work, and influence the cultural landscape they were in for good.

> **Teach**
> *But as for you, teach what accords with sound doctrine.*
> Titus 2:1
>
> **Why?**
> *. . . that the word of God may not be reviled.*
> Titus 2:5b
>
> *. . . so that an opponent may be put to shame, having nothing evil to say about us.*
> Titus 2:8b
>
> *Declare these things; exhort and rebuke with all authority. Let no one disregard you.*
> Titus 2:15

Clearly building strong families is key to impacting the culture. But how can this be done? We have a guide in Titus 2. In the passage Paul writes, "As for you, teach" (Titus 2:1). Regardless of what anyone else is doing you teach your children and families about the biblical standards for behavior. Paul also instructed believers to utilize older men and women (in Lot's case like Abraham and Sarah) in the training of children (Titus 2:2–3). The older people in the church are to teach the young how to treat their spouses and children (Titus 2:4–5). Paul even says we should teach youth how to work (Titus 2:9–10). Paul warns that when we fail in this mission the world ridicules the faith (Titus 2:5, 8, 15) as they ridiculed Lot (Genesis 19:9, 14) and many are ridiculing Christianity today.

Reach Your World

One of the problems of our time is we tend to focus on things we have no control over with little focus on that within our area of influence. For example, many are concerned with the decisions of the President, Congress, or the Supreme Court. Others are sidetracked by the latest exploits of the most popular reality television show star or favorite sports team. When it comes to the things over which we have control, our lives, our families, and interaction with our neighbors—we tend not to have time for that. It is important to consider that when we stand before the Lord one day that it is unlikely God will hold us accountable for the actions of the President, Congress, Supreme Court, or reality television stars. However, He is very likely to hold us accountable for our own behavior and influence (or lack of influence) upon our family, friends, and neighbors. May we focus our efforts on that which counts!

> *Now the word of the Lord came to Jonah the son of Amittai, saying, "Arise, go to Nineveh, that great city, and call out against it, for their evil has come up before me." But Jonah rose to flee to Tarshish from the presence of the Lord. He went down to Joppa and found a ship going to Tarshish. So he paid the fare and went down into it, to go with them to Tarshish, away from the presence of the Lord.*
>
> Jonah 1:1-3

JONAH THE HARDLINER

Another example from the Bible is Jonah. Jonah is the opposite of Lot. Jonah was a hardliner and he did not accommodate sin. The Bible introduces us to Jonah in 2 Kings 14:25. Though the king of Israel was wicked (2 Kings 14:24), Jonah prophesied about the border of Israel being restored. You get the feeling that Jonah really liked *his* people, and maybe disliked everyone else. You could call him a flag-waving prophet. Jonah is like many who are only concerned for the people that are like them. They only like those who look like, talk like, and act like themselves.

> **Your Mission**
> *Go into all the world and proclaim the gospel to the whole creation.*
> Mark 16:15

Love Only for His Own

Jonah was only interested in a familiar landscape. Yet, the believer is called to take God into all of the world. Jonah wanted to take the gospel to his own. The Bible shows us in Jonah 1 his mandated mission to "go to Nineveh, that great city, and call out against it, for their evil has come up before me" (Jonah 1:2). Jonah did not like Nineveh so he arose and went in the opposite direction. You cannot run from God, so while he was asleep on a ship a great storm arose. The wicked sailors asked him to pray, "that we may not perish" (Jonah 1:6). They learned that Jonah was the reason for the storm and confronted him (Jonah 1:7–8). They asked what they needed to do to calm the sea (Jonah 1:11). At this point, Jonah had a decision to make. He could stop running from God, and head back to Nineveh or he could die. Jonah would rather die than see God's grace come upon Nineveh. He instructed the men to throw him overboard, which they did. In one of the most controversial sections of the Bible, we learn of a big fish that God had prepared for Jonah. We are told that the creature swallowed Jonah. From its belly he prayed "But I with the voice of thanksgiving will sacrifice to you; what I have vowed I will pay. Salvation belongs to the LORD!" (Jonah 2:9). With that, the creature vomited Jonah out on dry land, and he went to Nineveh (Jonah 2:10; 3:1–2).

Jonah is like many who go to school or work with people entangled in sexual sin and loath them rather than pity their predicament. Should you find yourself unwilling to share the gospel with someone because of your dislike of them, you are operating with the attitude of Jonah. Many nonbelievers say that is exactly what Christians do today. In fact, they claim that Christians contradict themselves by overlooking other sins (sexual promiscuity, cohabitation, and divorce) and condemning those who have engaged in homosexual sin.

An Unempathetic Messenger
The Bible says that Jonah gave Nineveh a simple and brief message, "Yet forty days, and Nineveh shall be overthrown!" (Jonah 3:4) You get the feeling he did

> **Perceived Contradictions**[18]
>
> 4 out of 5 Evangelical Christians say homosexual relations between two consenting adults should be illegal
> *You shall not lie with a male as with a woman; it is an abomination.*
> Leviticus 18:22
>
> Only 3 out of 5 Evangelical Christians describe divorce as a sin.
> In another study only 39% of born again Christians embraced Jesus' teaching on divorce.
>
> *But I say to you that everyone who divorces his wife, except on the ground of sexual immorality, makes her commit adultery, and whoever marries a divorced woman commits adultery.*
> Matthew 5:32

not add a lot. It may have been the shortest message in history. There seem to have been no illustrations, no explanations, and no direction. It appears he had no concern at all for Nineveh, he just told them what was going to happen to Nineveh as a result of their sin. Yet, they repented. Instead of being pleased by the success of his efforts, Jonah became very angry (Jonah 4:1). He complained that he knew God was gracious, which was his initial reason for refusing to take the gospel to them. God then proceeded to give Jonah a message about grace. He caused a plant to grow that provided shade for Jonah (Jonah 4:6). Then He sent a worm to destroy the plant (Jonah 4:7) and the weather became more oppressive. Jonah was enraged (Jonah 4:9).

And the Lord said, "You pity the plant, for which you did not labor, nor did you make it grow, which came into being in a night and perished in a night. And should not I pity Nineveh, that great city, in which there are more than 120,000 persons who do not know their right hand from their left, and also much cattle?"

JONAH 4:10–11

God pointed out to Jonah that he was more concerned for a plant than the 120,000 people and numerous animals that lived in Nineveh (Jonah 4:10–11). The book of Jonah ends with a question, "And should not I pity Nineveh, that great city, in which there are more than 120,000 persons who do not know their right hand from their left, and also much cattle?" (Jonah 4:11).

LESSONS FROM JONAH

> In one study, less than 1 percent of Americans said they prayed for homosexuals.[19]

In our day, there is nothing more damaging to the mission of the church than the perceived hatred of Christians toward homosexuals. In some ways, our hatred for sin has resulted in us being ineffective in fighting it. When we find ourselves angry with those entangled in sexual sin (who do not know their right hand from their left), God asks of us, "Should I not pity them?" Jonah believed the right things about God. Jonah's beliefs were right, but his heart was wrong. It will take more than the right message to reach those today who struggle with sexual sin.

> *... The prayer of a righteous person has great power as it is working.*
>
> JAMES 5:16b

Pray Like Abraham

It will take prayer. Sadly, in one study less than 1 percent of Americans said they prayed for homosexuals.[20] It is likely we would see a difference in our effectiveness and attitude toward those entangled in sexual sin if we prayed more for them.

Contrast Jonah's attitude (and our own) with that of Abraham. It is obvious in Genesis 18 that the Lord knew Abraham would be disturbed by the destruction of Sodom. "The men ... looked down toward Sodom" and "the LORD said, 'Shall I hide from Abraham what I am about to do?'" (Genesis 18:16–17). Then the LORD told Abraham, "Because the outcry against Sodom and Gomorrah is great and their sin is very grave, I will go down to see whether they have done altogether according to the outcry that has come to me. And if not, I will know" (Genesis 18:20–21). Abraham knew what that meant. He knew enough about Sodom to know that they had sinned gravely, and that God was about to destroy them. Was he glad, as Jonah would have been over the destruction of Nineveh? No, not at all.

Which prayer are you praying?

JONAH IS ANGRY

> *... he was angry. And he prayed to the Lord and said, "O Lord, is not this what I said when I was yet in my country? That is why I made haste to flee to Tarshish; for I knew that you are a gracious God and merciful, slow to anger and abounding in steadfast love, and relenting from disaster. Therefore now, O LORD, please take my life from me, for it is better for me to die than to live."*
>
> JONAH 4:1b-3

Abraham had met some of the Sodomites when he rescued Lot. He had even met their king (Genesis 14). He was deeply troubled as he began to think about them being destroyed. He began to intercede on their behalf to God. Since he was talking directly to God you might say he engaged in a fervent prayer that is recorded over the course of ten verses. What a contrast between the prayer Abraham prayed to save Sodom, and the prayer Jonah prayed to destroy Nineveh! We would all do well to examine Abraham's prayer and ask ourselves, "Do I pray like Abraham for those entangled in sexual sin?"

Abraham Intercedes

Then Abraham drew near and said, "Will you indeed sweep away the righteous with the wicked? Suppose there are fifty righteous within the city. Will you then sweep away the place and not spare it for the fifty righteous who are in it? Far be it from you to do such a thing, to put the righteous to death with the wicked, so that the righteous fare as the wicked! Far be that from you! Shall not the Judge of all the earth do what is just?" ... Abraham answered and said, "Behold, I have undertaken to speak to the Lord, I who am but dust and ashes. Suppose five of the fifty righteous are lacking. Will you destroy the whole city for lack of five?" ... Again he spoke to him and said, "Suppose forty are found there." ... Then he said, "Oh let not the Lord be angry, and I will speak. Suppose thirty are found there." ... He said, "Behold, I have undertaken to speak to the Lord. Suppose twenty are found there." ... Then he said, "Oh let not the Lord be angry, and I will speak again but this once. Suppose ten are found there." ... when he had finished speaking to Abraham, and Abraham returned to his place.

Genesis 18:23-33

It is likely that Abraham's prayers for Sodom did not end in Genesis 18:33. In Genesis 19:27–28 we see "Abraham went early in the morning to the place where he had stood before the Lord. And he looked down toward Sodom and Gomorrah and toward all the land of the valley, and he looked and, behold, the smoke of the land went up like the smoke of a furnace." How do you feel when you see the smoldering results of destroyed lives and families? Abraham likely had tears in his eyes as he saw the smoke rise. Jonah had tears in his eyes because of a lack of smoke over Nineveh. Which prayer are you praying? Intercede like Abraham.

Have Empathy

God asked Jonah how he could have pity on a plant and have no pity on people that did not know their right hand from their left (Jonah 4) or right from wrong. God asks the same of us. Those who are entangled in sexual sin have probably been targets of attack for a long time.

Try to have empathy for them like Paul. To have empathy is to put yourself in the shoes of others and imagine what it would be like to experience their life. Paul did this with all kinds of people, as should we. In the gay and lesbian community the name Matthew Shepherd brings up a lot of emotion. Matthew Shepherd

> What would it be like to be laughed at for the way you walked or talked?

> **Paul the Empathizer**
>
> *For though I am free from all, I have made myself a servant to all, that I might win more of them. To the Jews <u>I became as a Jew</u>, in order to win Jews. To those under the law <u>I became as one under the law</u> (though not being myself under the law) that I might win those under the law. To those outside the law <u>I became as one outside the law</u> (not being outside the law of God but under the law of Christ) that I might win those outside the law. To the weak <u>I became weak</u>, that I might win the weak. <u>I have become all things to all people</u>, that by all means I might save some. I do it all for the sake of the gospel, that I may share with them in its blessings.*
>
> 1 Corinthians 9:19–23

was a gay student at the University of Wyoming who was murdered. At his funeral, members of the Westboro Baptist Church protested and indicated that Mr. Shepherd was treated as he deserved. This is why many who struggle with these issues believe that Christians hate them.

One of the best actions you can take is to have zero tolerance for bullying of those with these issues. If you work with youth, you want to prepare them to protect those who are attacked for whatever reason by their peers, as Jesus protected the woman caught in adultery (by asking "he who is without sin let him cast the first stone") (John 8). We want to protect them.

Three out of five teens that struggle with sexual issues say they do not feel safe[21] and actual or perceived sexual orientation is the most common reason students report being harassed by peers.[22] Those struggling with these issues face enough harassment without being attacked by the ones who can help them out of the snare in which they are entangled. It is important, as a Christian, that the people who struggle with sexual issues feel comfortable and safe around you. They have to have someone with whom they can discuss their struggles.

We cannot help people if they do not feel safe around us. If they are fearful they will not talk to us. If they do not talk to us we cannot help them. It is important to note that you are often speaking with someone who is struggling with these issues, though you may be unaware. Consider the number of Christian singers who have come out as gay or lesbian over the last few years. It appears that it would be a good idea for people to be able to come to the church and have a place to discuss their concerns about their sexual identity or we will see many more succumb to sexual sin.

> *And the Lord's servant must not be quarrelsome but kind to everyone, able to teach, patiently enduring evil, correcting his opponents with gentleness. God may perhaps grant them repentance leading to a knowledge of the truth.*
>
> 2 TIMOTHY 2:24–25

In 2 Timothy 2, Paul provided instruction to us about how to minister to others. He instructed us to be "kind" rather than "quarrelsome," "patiently enduring evil, correcting his opponents with gentleness." Our goal should be that "God may perhaps grant them repentance leading to the knowledge of truth, and they may come to their senses and escape from the snare of the devil, after being captured by him to do his will" (2 Timothy 2:25–26). The language describes well the problem of sexual sin and our role in rescuing people out of it. It is as if Paul had said, "Think about your goal as you minister to people. Have empathy for them realizing they have been ensnared by the devil. They are not to be looked upon with disdain but victims in need of rescue." This belies the importance of addressing this problem with wisdom. In *UnChristian* the authors describe the views of young adults about Christianity. They interviewed one young Christian who described a friend of his that was struggling with same-sex attraction and looking for answers. He was able to convince his friend to attend his youth group meeting. In the Bible study that night, the Youth Pastor joked that God created Adam and Eve not Adam and Steve, and made other such statements. The Christian interviewed stated that after the meeting his friend was no longer interested to see what Jesus might have to offer.[23]

When Christians do not handle these issues with wisdom there are consequences. Those who struggle with these issues are further ensnared and even other believers become disillusioned and no longer view their leaders as a resource.

Indeed, the data presented in *UnChristian* indicated that many young Christians are embarrassed by their church leaders and have not been equipped by them to effectively address these complicated problems.[24] If you are a church leader, your goal should be to create a safe environment. The gospel teaching about sexual sin is offensive enough to many without us clouding the issue with misguided statements.

Be Calm Like Paul

> *Now while Paul was waiting for them at Athens, his spirit was provoked within him as he saw that the city was full of idols.*
>
> Acts 17:16

In many ways it is only natural for Christians and non-Christians to be in conflict in a pluralistic society. We are not the first to face this challenge. It sounds like Paul had something like a layover in Athens recorded in Acts 17. He took the time to tour the city. As he did, he saw an abundance of idols all around him. "His spirit was provoked within him." It would have been easy to allow anger to boil over leading him to lash out at the people of Athens, but he did not.

Similarly, as you see the flaunting of sexual boundaries you too may find yourself deeply bothered and find the urge to lash out and even ridicule

> **Don't be like Jonah, embrace and always remember your mission**
>
> Ask yourself, "Why am I doing what I'm doing?"
>
> If I say or do _____, what am I likely to accomplish?

those who engage in this behavior. Some have done so, using harsh rhetoric, perhaps with an attitude like Jonah, further driving away the people they seek to help.

For example, one headline that ran in the *Huffington Post* quoted a pastor who said, "Put gays and lesbians in an electrified pen to kill them off."[25]

The Jonah who longed for the destruction of Nineveh would have probably loved the rhetoric. However, it seems to contradict the mission our Lord sent us upon, "Behold, I am sending you out as sheep in the midst of wolves, so be wise as serpents and innocent as doves" (Matthew 10:16). Some of the statements we make about those entangled in sexual sin are neither wise nor innocent or harmless.

It is unlikely the statement made by the pastor led to the changing of behavior and very likely it further alienated those who struggle with these sins. Anyone struggling with sexual sin in that congregation also clearly understood this is not a place I can find help for my struggles.

It is important to always ask yourself, "What do

> *If anyone thinks he is religious and does not bridle his tongue but deceives his heart, this person's religion is worthless.*
> James 1:26

I hope to accomplish?" before speaking about sensitive topics. Peter wrote, "But in your hearts honor Christ the Lord as holy, always being prepared to make a defense to anyone who asks you for a reason for the hope that is in you; yet do it with gentleness and respect" (1 Peter 3:15).

> *But Daniel resolved that he would not defile himself with the king's food, or with the wine that he drank. Therefore he asked the chief of the eunuchs to allow him not to defile himself.*
> DANIEL 1:8

DANIEL THE INFLUENCER

Lot was influenced by his landscape, while Jonah was hostile toward his. Daniel is a model for how one can enter a different landscape and be used by God to change it. He influenced the culture he was sent to toward God. How?

Real Resolve

Daniel lived at a time when everyone was "doing it." Everyone was eating the Babylonian food (Daniel 1), everyone was bowing to Nebuchadnezzar's image (Daniel 3), and perhaps everyone was ceasing to pray (Daniel 6). Similarly, it seems like everyone is looking at porn, cohabitating, divorcing, and engaging in same sex relationships. Many who are trying to obey God's instruction regarding sexual issues may complain that they are alone. When Elijah complained that he was the only one fol-

> For more on Daniel and his friends see *Surviving Culture* by E. Moody: published by Randall House.

lowing God, God replied that He had 7,000 who had not succumbed to Baal (1 Kings 19:18). In Daniel's day, Hananiah, Mishael, and Azariah were not going along. Everybody "isn't doing it" today either though everyone is struggling with something. One of the tactics Satan uses is to make it seem like everyone is doing something as a way to get others to just go along.

In the 1940s and 1950s the Kinsey report was released and it was a shock to society. The picture Kinsey painted was of a far more sexually promiscuous society where premarital sex, extramarital affairs, and homosexual behaviors were more prevalent than anyone ever thought. In Kinsey's samples, 50 percent

> *Therefore, as soon as all the peoples heard the sound of the horn, pipe, lyre, trigon, harp, bagpipe, and every kind of music, <u>all the peoples</u>, nations, and languages fell down and worshiped the golden image that King Nebuchadnezzar had set up.*
> Daniel 3:7

of women had engaged in premarital sex, and 26 percent of women had had an extramarital affair. Fifty percent of men had engaged in extramarital affairs. Further, 46 percent of males had engaged in both heterosexual and homosexual activities. He included a table in his book that indicated that 10 percent of the males in his sample were homosexual.[26] The image presented was that many (if not everyone) were engaging in sexually promiscuous behaviors. A closer look at the data reveals a somewhat different picture.

Anytime someone discusses a research study ask, "Where did you get your sample?" Kinsey's research did not involve a random sample. He might interview someone who had an affair and then ask if they knew others he could interview. He would then interview them and ask them whom they knew and on and on it went. His data on homosexuality was shocking to people. It is important to note that he conducted a lot of research on prisoners, and paid particular attention to people who had been convicted of sexual offenses. Of those he said reported being homosexual, 49.6 percent were incarcerated. The picture Kinsey painted was not an accurate picture of mainstream America.

I have often wondered how Kinsey's study impacted the attitudes of Americans about sex. The parents of Daniel, Hananiah, Mishael, and Azariah probably taught their children that God would always have a remnant that was not "doing it." But if not, they were to be firm in their resolve. They were not influenced by the culture around them. Daniel made plans and took steps to keep himself and his friends from being defiled by the king's food. When everyone else appeared to be doing it, Daniel and his friends looked for opportunities to escape the temptation they faced. As they did, whether it was refusing to eat defiled food, or to bow down to an image or praying after it had been forbidden—they showed those around them that there is a God worthy of one submitting their life to.

For Daniel, the majority of the youth from Judah would be like nominal Christians today who have been influenced by the culture around them. The Babylonians would be like those entangled in sexual sin or encouraging people to slide away in their culture. First, Daniel and his friends had to navigate how they would interact with both groups.

Daniel, Hananiah, Mishael, and Azariah had to figure out what they would do and would not do. When their names were changed to Babylonian names (Daniel 1:7) it appears they did not have a major problem. When they were told to eat the Babylonian food (Daniel 1:8), bow to the golden image (Daniel 3) or that they could not pray (Daniel 6), there was a problem.

Okay	Not Okay
• Changing to Babylonian names	• Eating Babylonian food
• Being with non-Jews	• Bowing to golden image
	• Cease praying

Here we are centuries later dealing with some of the same issues. Magistrates are told they must perform gay marriages or be prosecuted. Restaurateurs and florists are being told they must participate in gay marriages or face lawsuits. We would do well to study Daniel (and Esther and Nehemiah) for instruction about how to handle these situations. Clearly we cannot do that which defiles us (Daniel 1:8). However, neither can we retreat from the public sphere. We must go out of our way to be with those caught in these sins to create the opportunity for their exposure to Christ. Unlike Lot in Sodom, Daniel was able to have a firm resolve in the Babylonians landscape.

Real Concern
Unlike Jonah, Daniel had real concern for his landscape. This is especially clear in his interaction with Nebuchadnezzar. Nebuchadnezzar destroyed Daniel's homeland, killing the king's sons before their father's eyes were gouged out. If anyone ever had a reason to hate or withhold grace from another it was Daniel toward Nebuchadnezzar. Yet he kindly and respectfully shared truth with King Nebuchadnezzar. When Nebuchadnezzar was judged for his sin, Daniel did not celebrate. He mourned as Abraham had over Sodom. In the end, it appears that Nebuchadnezzar embraced Daniel's God and broke off his sins. How was Daniel able to be used of God to do this?

Perhaps Daniel looked past the sin of Nebuchadnezzar and the other Babylonians and saw them as people that God loved. Rather than seeing Nebuchadnezzar as a murderer or wicked dictator, Daniel appeared to see him as a person made in the image of God. Rather than seeing Arioch as someone who likely followed another god, Daniel appears to have seen him as one in authority (perhaps put there by God). Perhaps Daniel thought they engaged in the behavior they did because they did not know their right hand from their left (or right from wrong) as Nineveh did not. For us, rather than seeing someone as a pornographer, cohabiter, fornicator, adulterer, or homosexual we should see them as someone in need of the Lord and our love. Incidentally, is this not what Jesus did with the Samaritan woman at the well, Mary Magdalene, and so many others?

> *So God created man in his own image, in the image of God he created him; male and female he created them.*
> Genesis 1:27

Real Answers

It is not enough just to be kind to people though. Perhaps Lot even did that. We must provide them with answers. Nebuchadnezzar's entangling sin was pride and dabbling in sorcery. Throughout the book of Daniel you see Daniel giving answers even when Nebuchadnezzar did not really ask for them. For you, you will need to be prepared to answer questions about "Why do I feel these temptations, even after I have prayed for them to go away?" And, "Why am

> **Sowing Seeds**
>
> ... "*No wise men, enchanters, magicians, or astrologers can show to the king the mystery that the king has asked, but <u>there is a God</u> in heaven who reveals mysteries ...*
> Daniel 2:27-28
> *You, O king, the king of kings, to whom <u>the God of heaven</u> has given the kingdom ...*
> Daniel 2:37
> *... <u>the God of heaven</u> will set up a kingdom that shall never be destroyed ...*
> Daniel 2:44

I this way?" Too often, people entangled in sexual sin have not found answers from Christians and the church. We will look closer at this later.

Can I Change?

In Daniel 4, we see Nebuchadnezzar coming to grips with the consequences of a life of pride and mistreatment of others. You too will deal with people who experience the consequence of their own behavior. When they do, many wonder if they can change. Daniel gave Nebuchadnezzar the answer though he was not quite ready to follow the advice. You too must be prepared to help others find their way out of this sin, as we will see later. Because of the life Daniel lived, God changed the landscape of Babylon. Let us look for ways God might use us to impact our own landscape.

Maybe you are reading this booklet and you get it. You are ready to do what you can to help those entangled in sin. Where do you start? Consider the relationship of Nebuchadnezzar and Daniel. It is important to realize, it did not just happen. I think Daniel was intentional about cultivating a relationship with Nebuchadnezzar and making each conversation with him count. I think Daniel had spent hours praying for Nebuchadnezzar.

If we are going to do something about the sexual landscape in the U.S., we must be intentional about seeking relationships with and praying for those entangled in sexual sin. Sadly, it seems Christians recognize that sexual sin is a problem, but we do not know what to do

> *Therefore, O king, let my counsel be acceptable to you: break off your sins by practicing righteousness, and your iniquities by showing mercy to the oppressed, that there may perhaps be a lengthening of your prosperity.*
> Daniel 4:27

about it. For example, in one study although most Christians report being concerned about homosexuality, only 10 percent reported doing anything non-political about it.

Part of the problem may be that many Christians today do not even think they can be friends with a homosexual. How will they and others who are entangled in sexual sin, ever learn anything about Jesus?[27]

> **Befriend Like Jesus**
> And as Jesus reclined at table in the house, behold, many <u>tax collectors and sinners</u> came and were reclining with Jesus and his disciples. And when the Pharisees saw this, they said to his disciples, "<u>Why does your teacher eat with tax collectors and sinners?</u>"
> Matthew 9:10-11
>
> And as he reclined at table in his house, many <u>tax collectors and sinners</u> were reclining with Jesus and his disciples, for there were many who followed him.
> Mark 2:15
>
> And the Pharisees and their scribes grumbled at his disciples, saying, "<u>Why do you eat and drink with tax collectors and sinners?</u>"
> Luke 5:30

Also, consider that Jesus was often attacked for being a "friend of sinners." Look at the attitude Jesus had toward people that were entangled in sin. He clearly loved them. People complained that Jesus was always with tax collectors and sinners. The word sinners probably referred to many entangled in sexual sin. The religious leaders would not eat with sinners. One reason was they could not be sure the sinner had given a tithe on the food that was eaten. Jesus indicated they should not have allowed that to lead to neglect of the weightier matters.

Consider Paul's instruction about associating with immoral people.

I wrote to you in my letter not to associate with sexually immoral people—not at all meaning the sexually immoral of this world, or the greedy and swindlers, or idolaters, since then you would need to go out of the world. But now I am writing to you not to associate with anyone who bears the name of brother if he is guilty of sexual immorality or greed, or is an idolater, reviler, drunkard, or swindler— not even to eat with such a one.

1 CORINTHIANS 5:9–11

> *Woe to you, scribes and Pharisees, hypocrites! For you tithe mint and dill and cumin, and have neglected the weightier matters of the law: justice and mercy and faithfulness. These you ought to have done, without neglecting the others.*
> Matthew 23:23

Paul explained clearly to us that when he instructed Christians to not associate with sexually immoral people, he was referring to those who bear the name of a brother. In fact, he wanted Christians to associate with those of the world and noted that you have to; otherwise, you would have to go out of the world. We need the right approach to reach them. We know from research that those who struggle with same-sex attraction long for same-sex friends who will love them in a nonsexual way, like David loved Jonathan and Ruth loved Naomi. Will you be that kind of friend to someone struggling with sexual sin? While not allowing them to become dependent upon you, you can help defeat the feeling of isolation that often comes with this struggle.[28]

The Right Approach

A good example for us to follow is found in John 4 where Jesus interacted with a Samaritan woman at a well. She was entangled in sexual sin and it appears Jesus went to the well in an attempt to meet her and those like her (John 4:3–4). For us, this can be going to school, work, a coffee shop, the gym, or some place we know we will interact with others who need Jesus.

A few years ago a Christian college professor was on a bus when a passenger asked him what kind of work he did. After he told the passenger about his work and she realized he was a Christian, she said something about how he would not like her very much since she was a lesbian. This led him to think about what to say to the woman on the bus.[29] His thoughts sparked many of the ideas that follow. He encouraged us to look for opportunities to be Jesus to people wherever we find them. As you begin to minister with those who struggle with these issues, think about how you look to them and how you communicate with them.

Build Relationships

Whereas other Jews would have avoided or ignored the Samaritan woman at the well, Jesus approached her and said, "Give me a drink" (John 4:7). To us this may have seemed to be rude. However, to her, she was surprised that a Jew (much less a rabbi) would take the time to speak to her, let alone drink water with her. Her surprise is seen when she reminded him, "'How is it that you, a Jew, ask for a drink from me, a woman of Samaria?' (For Jews have no dealings with Samaritans)" (John 4:9). This would be like a person who is entangled in sexual sin saying, "Hey, Christians don't speak to people like me," after asking about having coffee or a meal together. When Jesus engaged her, He was allowing her to tell Him her story.

Tell me your story

When someone says, "You wouldn't like me I'm gay" or because of another sexual sin there are clearly some assumptions, and perhaps some experiences behind that statement. We might respond by asking them "What is behind that statement?" or "Help me understand why you feel that way" or simply "Tell me your story." People want to talk about themselves and be understood. You will be different if you give someone the opportunity to tell you about their experience. You will also learn from them and even if you are unable to help them, their story will help prepare you to help others.

> ... *be quick to hear, slow to speak, slow to anger.*
>
> James 1:19b

> *Walk in wisdom toward outsiders, making the best use of the time.*
>
> Colossians 4:5

Listen

In *UnChristian* the researchers noted that many nonbelievers say Christians do not listen very well.[30] Perhaps we are so eager to share the truth that we do not take the time to hear what others have to say. Taking the time to listen is a prerequisite to teaching. Maybe we are unwilling to take the time required to listen. Jesus listened to the Samaritan woman at the well. She talked about spiritual issues and eventually her sexual life. When you listen to people you are investing in them. It is a way of letting them know that they are important to you. You will learn more about them, and that will put you into a better position to help them. You are taking the time to learn about the person, and they may be gauging you to see if you can handle their problem. In doing so, some people tell very personal things they may not have shared with others.

Put Yourself in Their Shoes

Often we are unaware of how those entangled in sexual sin have been treated by so called Christians. As you listen to someone it is important to put yourself into his or her shoes. What might it be like to have the experiences they have had? How might that have felt? Paul said he did that as he worked with others. So we listen with them and identify with them in order to try to help them. Note, that to put yourself in the shoes of others does not mean you are condoning their behavior. Paul was not condoning the sins of the lawless or the Judaizers, but he did this so that some of them might be saved (1 Corinthians 9).

A sower went out to sow his seed. And as he sowed . . .

Luke 8:5

Sow Seeds

Earlier we looked at how the attitude Daniel held is helpful as we try to reach those entangled in sexual sin. Nebuchadnezzar sought out magicians and sorcerers for answers to his dreams. Watch how Daniel seemed to always be looking for opportunities to share with Nebuchadnezzar that the source of real wisdom was God.

How many seeds did Daniel (and his friends) plant with Nebuchadnezzar?

. . . No wise men, enchanters, magicians, or astrologers can show to the king the mystery that the king has asked, but <u>there is a God</u> in heaven who reveals mysteries. . . .

Daniel 2:27–28

You, O king, the king of kings, to whom <u>the God of heaven</u> has given the kingdom . . .

Daniel 2:37

. . . <u>the God of heaven</u> will set up a kingdom that shall never be destroyed . . .

Daniel 2:44

> *... <u>A great God</u> has made known to the king what shall be after this. The dream is certain, and its interpretation sure.*
>
> Daniel 2:45

> *... <u>our God whom we serve is able</u> to deliver us from the burning fiery furnace ...*
>
> Daniel 3:17

> *... break off your sins by practicing righteousness, and your iniquities by showing mercy to the oppressed ...*
>
> Daniel 4:27

> *... seven periods of time shall pass over you, until you know that the Most High rules the kingdom of men and gives it to whom he will.*
>
> Daniel 4:32b

You might be looking for opportunities to share about the love of God, and the help He gives.

You might say,

> There is a God who forgives sin, and moves it as far as the east is from the west.
> There is a God who can remake the most marred life.
> There is a God who builds families to love one other and survive and thrive in the midst of great difficulty.

Daniel spent a lot of time listening to Nebuchadnezzar, but when he got the opportunity he succinctly planted seed. Be prepared to talk about grace, the Bible on sexual sin, and the biblical description of a family. When you speak, make it count.

Realize There Will Not Be a Quick Fix

Perhaps many Christians have gotten the idea over the years that a quick sharing of the gospel with a stranger often leads to an immediate change in life. Sometimes this is the case, but increasingly because of the deficits people have about Christian teaching (in the autumn) this is less likely. In the work of *UnChristian*, many noted that they see Christians as a kind of spiritual headhunter only interested in people if they respond to the gospel. Some expressed disbelief after Christians who seemed to have befriended them abandoned them after they did not immediately positively respond to the gospel.[31] For many who are entangled in this kind of sin it will take a lot of time for them to come to Christ and be changed just like it took decades of work with Nebuchadnezzar. One would think that Nebuchadnezzar would have begun to follow Jehovah after his experience in Daniel 2 where his dream was revealed and interpreted. Though Nebuchadnezzar took steps toward God, he took two steps back when he made his image and demanded that others bow down to it. The incident created another opportunity for Nebuchadnezzar to follow Jehovah as he saw God in the fiery furnace (Daniel 3). Yet, he continued to stray. It is only after the intervention recorded in Daniel 4, where Nebuchadnezzar lost his capacity to think, that he appears to have repented and to have followed God. Prepare for the long haul if you plan to minister to people entangled in these kinds of sins.

Build a Bridge
Each time Daniel interacted with Nebuchadnezzar he was building a bridge. You too are trying to build bridges. Consider the conversion of Rosaria Champagne Butterfield, who refers to her own conversion as a train wreck. It did not come easy or quickly, but it did come. As a tenured Syracuse University Professor of English and women's studies she says she despised Christians. She set out to attack Jesus, Republican politics, and the patriarchy with an article in her newspaper about Promise Keepers back in 1997. As a result, she received a lot of hate mail and fan mail though there was a letter from Ken Smith of Syracuse Reformed Presbyterian Church with which she did not know what to do. He asked her questions about how she came to her conclusions and what she thought of God. He did not argue with her and she did not know what to do with the letter. It was the beginning of a two-year journey where Ken and his wife brought the church to her. They all became friends as they exchanged meals, books, and talked openly about sexuality and politics. She also noted that she had never heard anyone pray like Ken did where he seemed to thank God for everything. Eventually

Rosario began to read the Bible and she did so many times in many translations. One day a transgendered friend warned her that the Bible was changing her. As a former Presbyterian minister the friend offered to pray for her. She kept reading the Bible. One Sunday morning she left the bed of her lesbian lover and went to church and as she contemplated what she heard she questioned who she really was. Some time later, on an ordinary day, after a lot of prayers she came to Jesus and surrendered her life to Him.[32] May we see more Ken Smith's (and Daniel's). The result will be more Rosaria Champagne Butterfield's. More lives radically changed by Christ.

> **For videos and more from Rosaria Champagne Butterfield go to**
> **http://rosariabutterfield.com**

For the wrath of God is revealed from heaven against all ungodliness and unrighteousness of men, who by their unrighteousness suppress the truth.

ROMANS 1:18

Proclaim Truth

As you interact with others around sexual issues you will find there is much confusion and misinformation. One of the tools the devil uses is to suppress the truth and keep people in darkness. Jesus has told us that knowing the truth leads to freedom. It is critical that you equip yourself to proclaim the truth about Scripture, science, and sin.

Proclaim the truth, not stereotypes or opinions. Too many have gotten off track as they have free-lanced about how to address sexual issues. For example, some have feared the arts and tried to push "manly" sports on children who have enjoyed other activities apparently forgetting some of the "manliest" men in Scripture were accomplished artists (consider David the accomplished harpist). Our role is to proclaim the truth clearly with the right attitude.

> *And you will know the truth, and the truth will set you free.*
> John 8:32

THE TRUTH ABOUT SCRIPTURE

Interestingly, many today try to suppress the truth of Scripture by saying the times have changed and so the Scripture no longer applies. You can get a good sense of some of the arguments put forth by examining books like Gene Robinson's *God Believes in Love*.[33] It is not my goal here to examine or discuss these arguments. You can find a thorough examination of passages addressing sexual sin in R. A. Gangon's *The Bible and Homosexual Practice: Texts and Hermeneutics*,[34] which I highly recommend.

> *Do your best to present yourself to God as one approved, a worker who has no need to be ashamed, rightly handling the word of truth.*
> 2 Timothy 2:15

> ### The Bible on Sex
>
> **Pornography**—*But I say to you that everyone who looks at a woman with lustful intent has already committed adultery with her in his heart.*
> Matthew 5:28
>
> **Premarital Sex**—*Let marriage be held in honor among all, and let the marriage bed be undefiled, for God will judge the sexually immoral and adulterous.*
> Hebrews 13:4
>
> **Extramarital Sex**—*You shall not commit adultery.*
> Exodus 20:14
>
> **Homosexual Sex**—*You shall not lie with a male as with a woman; it is an abomination.*
> Leviticus 18:22

If you are even a casual reader of the Bible, you can see throughout a description of appropriate and inappropriate sexual behavior. From the beginning until the end of the Bible, we are presented with a choice between living a God-oriented or self-oriented life. We see this in the Ten Commandments (Exodus 20), the *Shema* (Deuteronomy 6), later in the hymn to Christ in Philippians 2, and at the end of the Bible in Revelation 22:13. To follow Christ is to die to yourself (no longer living for yourself but for God), as Christ explained in Mark 8:34-37. Paul noted that to follow Christ is to take your thoughts captive (2 Corinthians 10:4–5) and to reorient your whole life away from self and onto God (Galatians 2:19–20).[35]

What does this have to do with sexual sin?

Everything. When one decides to follow Christ, they decide to live God's way, regardless of the urges they may feel. The result is a willingness to pray and live, not my will but Your will be done.

The Truth About Science

Today it seems that there is a concerted effort to silence any voice that contradicts the conventional wisdom about the current sexual landscape. For example, earlier a study published by Dr. Mark Regnerus was discussed. The study ("How different are the adult children of parents who have same-sex relationships? Findings from the New Family Structures Study") examined families, including those headed by homosexual parents. It was published in the peer reviewed journal *Social Science Research*.[36] Whereas previous studies had examined the viewpoint of parents, this study examined the viewpoint of children about their family environment.

Interestingly, this led to a firestorm of controversy. Though Regnerus posted his data on his website (www.markregnerus.com) for anyone to see (and reanalyze) he was ridiculed in the *New Yorker,* which referred to the study as "A Faulty 'Gay Parenting' Study"[37] and the *Slate* which published an article on his work entitled "The Shamelessness of Professor Mark Regnerus."[38] Dr. Regnerus attended Calvin College as an undergraduate, which is a Christian college, and he is a practicing Catholic. This led the *New York Times* to question whether he should be conducting such research since his faith might impact how he conducts research in an article entitled "Sociologist's paper raises questions about the role of faith in scholarship."[39] There are many things that motivate scholars. For example, Dr. Simon LeVay, the author of *Gay, Straight, and the Reason Why: The Science of Sexual Orientation*[40] has reported that he was motivated to do some of his work after the death of his same-sex lover. Yet, the *New York Times* did not express similar concern when describing Dr. LeVay's work. At the heart of true researchers is a desire to know the truth regardless of where it may lead. Though a researcher may be motivated to do their work because of their experience or interests that does not have to indicate bias will result. Researchers are rarely activists.

Perhaps the clearest example of suppression of truth is what is happening in the debate over therapy for those who would like to change their sexual orientation. Clearly, some have been harmed by these approaches and some of these interventions have been misused. But it seems like science has been lost in the debate. For many years if you visited the website of the American Psychological Association you would see the question "Can therapy change sexual orientation?" The response was "No . . . Homosexuality is not an illness and does not require treatment and is not changeable."[42]

Jones and Yarhouse (2011) have noted that this seems like an unscientific answer. Can we scientifically know that anything is never possible? The message today is, if you want to change, you cannot and you should not. However, dozens of studies over the decades suggest significant change in sexual preference by at least some of those seeking to change by using professional psychotherapy or religious approaches.[43] Some of these studies are very substantial. In fact, in "Ex-Gays?" a 6-7 year longitudinal study of Christian ministries demonstrates changes as a result of Christian interventions.[44]

It seems there is an unwillingness to look at the

Some Studies Showing Some Sexual Change

W. Freeman, & R. G. Meyer (1975). A behavioral alteration of sexual preferences in the human male. *Behavior Therapy*, 6, 206-212.

L. Hatterer (1970). *Changing heterosexuality in the male: Treatment for men troubled by homosexuality.* New York: McGraw-Hill.

J. Munzer (1965). Treatment of the homosexual in group psychotherapy. *Topical Problems of Psychotherapy*, 5, 164-169.

E. M. Pattison, & M. Pattison (1980). "Ex-gays": Religiously mediated change in homosexuals. *American Journal of Psychiatry*, 137, 1553-1562.

R. A. Truax, & G. Tourney (1971). Male homosexuals in group psychotherapy. *Diseases of the Nervous System*, 32, 707-711.

data in an unbiased fashion. Consider what happened to Dr. Robert Spitzer, considered by many to be the father of American psychiatry. In 2003, Dr. Spitzer published a controversial study entitled, "Can some gay men and lesbians change their sexual orientation: 200 participants reporting a change from homosexual to heterosexual orientation?" The study was published in the peer-reviewed journal, *Archives of Sexual Behavior*.[45]

In the 1970s, Spitzer was a leader in the revision of the third edition of the Diagnostic and Statistical Manual of Mental Disorders that is used by mental health professionals to diagnose mental illness. In his leadership as chair of the American Psychiatric Association's Taskforce on Nomenclature and Statistics in the 1970s, he led the successful effort to remove homosexuality from the Diagnostic and Statistical Manual. Therefore, no one would accuse him of being a crusading evangelical or an enemy of the gay and lesbian community, until he published his article in October of 2003. After publication of the paper, many were critical of Spitzer's paper and he retracted the study in 2012.

Lest one think the study were thrown together with little thought it is important to follow the progression. On May 9, 2001, at the annual meeting of the American Psychiatric Association, Dr. Spitzer delivered his controversial paper. His findings indicated it was possible for highly motivated individuals to successfully change their sexual orientation from homosexual to heterosexual. This is the paper submitted to the *Archives of Sexual Behavior*. Some noted in the edition that study was published, that it was good to take the politics out of the controversial issue and simply examine it scientifically. In the edition of the journal where the article was published, there were 26 responses to Dr. Spitzer's article. Some praised his work as an opportunity to soberly examine a highly emotional issue. Some accused him of essentially being a Nazis. Finally, Dr. Spitzer wrote a response standing by his findings. After nearly a decade of controversy, Dr. Spitzer retracted his study and apologized for it.[46]

A few years after Spitzer's study was published, Christian psychologists Stanton Jones and Mark Yarhouse attempted to find a publisher for their work "Ex-gays? A longitudinal study of religiously mediated change to sexual orientation." No non-religious publishers would publish the material.[47] Jones and Yarhouse finally published it with the Christian publisher, Intervarsity Press. Though the work is scientifically based, and findings from it published in the peer reviewed *Journal of Sex and Marital Therapy*, CNN's Sanjay Gupta seemed to dismiss the work because the researchers "work at religious universities" and because "gay advocacy blogs have also disputed the findings."[48]

The result has been two-fold. First, those who struggle with same-sex attraction and would like to change are left with the impression that there is no hope of change. The second result is that researcher's have received the not so subtle message that one dare not present data contrary to conventional wisdom on sexual behavior lest they destroy their career. In the past, many secular therapists tried to help those who struggled with sexual issues, like Columbia University educated psychiatrist Lawrence Hatterer who wrote *Changing the Homosexual Male* back in 1970.[49] But the days of secular therapists helping those who struggle with sexual issues may be over. Spitzer appears to have retracted his research after being convinced that efforts to help (or force) people to change was damaging. No doubt some of those efforts have been misguided and harmful. But, it is frightening to see an area essentially removed from scientific inquiry. What does this mean for you?

Like it or not truth is being suppressed so you must begin to think like a scientist. When you hear about a study in the media, you have to ask the right questions about it and examine it. Ask: Who was in the sample? How was the sample obtained? What exactly did they find in the study? What are the implications of the study? What does the Bible say about this issue?

But in your hearts honor Christ the Lord as holy, always being prepared to make a defense to anyone who asks you for a reason for the hope that is in you; yet do it with gentleness and respect.

1 PETER 3:15

Think Like a Scientist

For example, today the conventional wisdom is that people engage in sexual behaviors because they were made this way. On February 24, 1992, the cover of *Newsweek* had a baby on it with the caption, "Is this child gay?"[50] The article was based upon research published in 1991, in the *Archives of General Psychiatry*.[51] The results seemed to indicate there was evidence suggesting a genetic link to homosexuality.[52] The media latched upon the study and it helped shape the current sexual landscape. Instead of accepting such a study at face value, take the time to examine it. The first questions to ask are who is in the sample and how was the sample obtained?

The Sample (Who is in the sample and how was it obtained?)

In this highly publicized study, the researchers wanted to study siblings to see if there was a relationship between genetics and sexual orientation. The researchers were especially interested in identical twins (monozygotic) because they have the same genetic components, coming from the same sperm and the same egg. You can even see the genetic similarities of identical twins (same eye color, hair color). Dr. Stanton Jones, the Provost of Wheaton College, has noted that the sample was obtained by targeting the gay and lesbian population through the advertising used. This led to a nonrandom sample that might be more motivated to respond in a biased manner. Why does this matter? Suppose you were to stand outside of a church that had a core belief that the Bible is the Word of God and asked whether one agreed more with the biblical account of creation or the theory of evolution. Would you be able to generalize the results to the rest of the city, state, and country? It is likely that your sample would be biased, which would impact the results making it difficult to generalize the data obtained outside of the church to the general population.

> **Questions to Ask About Research**
> Who is in the sample?
> How was the sample obtained?
> What exactly did they find?
> Has the study been replicated?
> What are the implications?
> What does the Bible say about this issue?

THE STUDY (What exactly did they find?)

After you examine the sample, look at what the researchers actually found. In this case, the researchers reported probandwise concordance rates of 52 percent for identical twins, 22 percent for fraternal (dizygotic) twins, 9 percent for non-twin siblings, and 11 percent for adopted siblings. What does that mean? It is hard to know unless you understand probandwise concordance. In the case of this study, the media focused on the results for identical twins and it appears many thought the results indicated that if one twin were homosexual, 52 percent of the time the other twin was homosexual. This was a misunderstanding of probandwise concordance. Probandwise concordance is computed by taking the number of matches and dividing them by the number of matches and the number of nonmatching twin pairs. In essence, if a set of identical twins were both homosexual, they were counted twice.

All of this can be confusing so it might be easier to look at exactly what Bailey and Pillard found. In the case of the identical twins, Bailey and Pillard had 41 pairs of twins (40 sets of twins and 1 set of triplets). They had 13 pairs of twins where both twins were gay, and all 3 of the triplets were gay. They had 27 pairs where only one twin was gay. In other words, when one twin (or triplet) was gay 34 percent of the time the other twin (or triplet) was gay.[53] When you think about it like that, the results are not nearly as impressive, especially with a biased sample.

Stanton further noted that if we were looking for a genetic component for same sex attraction, we would expect a higher rate of concordance. For example, for monozygotic (identical) twins, if one twin has blue eyes, 100 percent of the time the other twin will have blue eyes.[54]

THE SECOND STUDY (Was the study replicated?)

Researchers always try to replicate their study. In other words, if a researcher conducted one study that indicated a medication was effective, more studies would be conducted before the medication were put on the market to make sure the one study was not an anomaly. Bailey and Pillard set out to replicate their study with a more diverse sample. They found the Australian Twin Registry that could serve as a random sample. This registry includes every twin born in Australia. Bailey surveyed them. With the more representative sample Bailey found a probandwise concordance rate of 20 percent for identical twins. In other words out of 27 identical twins only 3 out of 27 or 11 percent consisted of both twins being gay. Therefore, the study was not replicated. Bailey and colleagues noted, "This suggests concordances from prior studies were inflated due to concordance dependent ascertainment bias." In other words, our previous results were a result of a biased sample. Bailey also noted that the new study did not provide statistically significant support for a genetic basis for homosexual orientation. This study went largely unreported in the media.[55]

WHAT ARE THE IMPLICATIONS?

To date the research is not as supportive as has been portrayed about a genetic cause for homosexuality and other sexual sins. However, in one study 88 percent of gay men and 68 percent of lesbians said they had no choice at all about their sexual orientation.[56]

You will likely be unsuccessful in convincing many that their sexual desires do not have a genetic cause. Further, you may lose credibility if you tell someone their behavior is a choice because they may be thinking, "I did not choose to be this way." Perhaps, this is not where we should be focusing our attention. It is unwise to overly focus on what causes same sex attraction. We do not focus on what causes opposite sex attraction to someone who is not ones spouse or what causes a number of other urges. Who can determine what is genetic and what are urges the Bible refers to as "the flesh?" I do not think it is helpful to argue about causation. As C. S. Lewis said, "I take it for certain that physical satisfaction of homosexual desires is sin. This leaves the homosexual no worse off than any normal person who is, for whatever reason, prevented from marrying... Our speculations on the cause of the abnormality are not what matters and we must be content with ignorance. The disciples were not told why (in terms of efficient cause) the man was born blind (John 9:1-3): only the final cause that the works of God should be made manifest in him. This suggests that in homosexuality, as in every other tribulation, those works can be made manifest: i.e. that every disability conceals a vocation, if only we can find it."[57]

WHAT DOES THE BIBLE SAY ABOUT THIS?

The research to this point is not as strong as has been portrayed regarding genetic causation of sexual desire but what does the Bible say? The Bible makes it clear that everything changed when sin entered the world. The picture of the way things were meant to be is found in Genesis 1-2. The picture of the way things are because of sin is found in Genesis 3. When sin entered the world it spread into our genes, our brains, it impacted everything.

> *Therefore, just as sin came into the world through one man, and death through sin, and so death spread to all men because all sinned—*
> ROMANS 5:12

The fall left us with some pretty bad genes. Some people's genes make them more susceptible to cancer; others heart disease or Alzheimer's disease. There is good research pointing to how ones genes make them more susceptible to substance abuse, depression, and anger problems.[58] If someone learns they have a genetic predisposition to an illness or a problem, most do not say, "I guess I'm destined to have breast cancer." Consider the steps Angeline Jolie took after learning she had the gene making her susceptible to breast cancer. Some who have a genetic marker for Alzheimer's disease take the time to learn another language, or to work on crossword puzzles daily to delay onset or prevent the disease. Over the last few years we have learned that it is the choices one makes that can lead to a different outcome in life even if they are genetically predisposed toward an illness, problem, or even a particular sin.

WHY AM I THIS WAY?

There has been much in the media indicating that sexual differences are the result of differences within the brain. Perhaps the most influential study is one conducted by neurobiologist Simon LeVay at the Salk Institute in California that was published in 1991.[59]

LeVay's goal was to compare the brains of heterosexual and homosexual men. He concluded that an area of the hypothalamus called the interstitial nucleus of the anterior hypothalamus 3 (INAH3) was larger in heterosexual men than homosexual men and heterosexual women.

Again, Stanton Jones helps us by taking a closer look at this study. An examination of the study indicates that there were problems with the sample that was obtained from the Bay area of California. Nineteen of the men were assigned the designation of homosexual based on identification by their doctors in their medical charts. Sixteen of the men were assumed to be heterosexual because there was no mention of sexual orientation in their medical charts. All of the men classified as homosexual had died from AIDS and 6 of the men classified as heterosexual had died from AIDS. A major problem is that it is not clear that those classified as homosexual were truly homosexual and those classified as heterosexual were truly heterosexual. Further, since a majority of the sample died from AIDS (all of those classified as homosexual) they would have been treated with strong medications. Jones mentions that a side effect of at least one medication may be the suppression of testosterone. Further, the study has yet to be replicated.[60]

In follow up studies on INAH3 by William Byne

and colleagues, it was concluded that sexual orientation cannot be predicted on INAH3 volume alone. Byne also noted if there are differences they are not proof of determination of sexual orientation.[61] Jones and Kwee (2005) explained it like this. If there is a structure difference between homosexual and heterosexuals it may well be a result of the sexual behavior.[62]

Many people who struggle with sexual sin sincerely believe they are different from others. Indeed, sometimes their friends and family will point out that in some cases they talk, walk, and think differently than others. There is research that supports this. For example, in one study participants were able to look at a photo for 50 milliseconds and correctly judge the sexual orientation of the person 60 percent of the time.[63] This would seem to indicate that people who engage in certain sexual behaviors are different in some way.

> *Flee from sexual immorality. Every other sin a person commits is outside the body, but the sexually immoral person sins against his own body.*
>
> 1 CORINTHIANS 6:18

What Does the Bible Say?

What could be the explanation? Interestingly, the Bible points to the changes a person undergoes as they "feed the flesh." Jesus said to lust is the equivalent of adultery indicating there is a spiritual consequence of lust. Studies also indicate there is a physical impact. We know from studies on individuals that the viewing of pornography has an impact upon the brain. Paul said in Romans 1 that as one continues to lust, God gives them over to a reprobate mind. This appears to indicate that in addition to a hardened spiritual condition one can experience physical impact upon their body as a result of the thoughts and fantasies in which they engage. Paul wrote about sexual sin saying, every sin a person commits is outside of the body but he who sins sexually, sins against his body. This indicates to us the physical nature of sin.[64]

Sin Impacts Your Brain

The truth is that everyone has urges that should we embrace would be a violation of Scripture, and they would have an impact upon our body. For example, some have a strong urge to drink alcohol or ingest other substances. If they submit to that urge (or become a slave to the flesh) their behavior will impact their body, especially their brain. When one uses such substances the myelin sheath that protects axons and dendrites in the brain erodes. The result is damage to the neurons or cells of the brain making it more difficult for one to learn and in some cases leading to other behavioral problems. The bottom line is that as one engages in sin, it impacts the brain. Interestingly, LeVay acknowledged we are uncertain about causation (if the brain is different) when he talked about his own study saying, "we don't know if the differences I found were there at birth or if they appeared later."[65] If there truly are differences in the brain, it may be that the behavior caused them. Is this not what Romans 1 says?

> *Therefore God gave them up in the lusts of their hearts to impurity, to the dishonoring of their bodies among themselves, because they exchanged the truth about God for a lie and worshiped and served the creature rather than the Creator, who is blessed forever! Amen.*
>
> *For this reason God gave them up to dishonorable passions. For their women exchanged natural relations for those that are contrary to nature; and the men likewise gave up natural relations with women and were consumed with passion for one another, men committing shameless acts with men and receiving in themselves the due penalty for their error.*
>
> *And since they did not see fit to acknowledge God, God gave them up to a debased mind to do what ought not to be done.*
>
> ROMANS 1:24-28

Taking the time to really look at research, even that with claims contrary to Scripture, is helpful. The truth often emerges.

Or do you not know that the unrighteous will not inherit the kingdom of God? Do not be deceived: neither the sexually immoral, nor idolaters, nor adulterers, nor men who practice homosexuality, nor thieves, nor the greedy, nor drunkards, nor revilers, nor swindlers will inherit the kingdom of God. <u>And such were some of you</u>. But you were washed, you were sanctified, you were justified in the name of the Lord Jesus Christ and by the Spirit of our God.

1 Corinthians 6:9-11

The Truth About Sin

The truth is that God has been saving and changing people who have been entangled in sexual sin for thousands of years. Paul made this clear in 1 Corinthians 6. But how? It is the same process that David, Rahab, and so many others have undertaken. For a fuller picture of how see "First Aid for Your Emotional Hurts: Sexual Issues" published by Randall House.

You Can Be Changed

Have mercy on me, O God, according to your steadfast love; according to your abundant mercy blot out my transgressions. Wash me thoroughly from my iniquity, and cleanse me from my sin!

Psalm 51:1-2

Repent

The first step is for one to repent. A repentant person will make Psalm 51 their own. Like David they will pray "Have mercy on me, O God, according to your steadfast love; according to your abundant mercy blot out my transgressions" (Psalm 51:1). "Wash me thoroughly from my iniquity, and cleanse me from my sin!" (Psalm 51:2). "Purge me with hyssop, and I shall be clean; wash me, and I shall be whiter than snow" (Psalm 51:7). "Hide your face from my sins, and blot out all my iniquities" (Psalm 51:9). "Deliver me from bloodguiltiness, O God, O God of my salvation, and my tongue will sing aloud of your righteousness" (Psalm 51:14). They will acknowledge that they like all others have sinned, and that we are to submit every area of our lives to the Lord, including sexual behavior. Repentance is just the beginning.

> *Create in me a clean heart, O God, and renew a right spirit within me.*
>
> Psalm 51:10

Create in Me

The repentant person commits to living a different kind of life. Rather than allowing themselves to see temptation, be enticed by it, and engage in lust; they flee from sexual sin. As they do, they become stronger and more capable of resisting. However, with sexual sin, like all other sin, one must deny oneself of the passions that war against the soul. When faced with the temptation of Potiphar's wife, Joseph did not hang around. He fled. This leads to hard choices like where one will live and who one will associate with. The person who is entangled in sexual sin may find it necessary to move to another city or region of the country because of cues and triggers they encounter as they are around people or places where they once engaged in an entangling sin. This is the kind of thing Jesus referred to in Matthew 5:27-30. He indicated that one makes hard choices to avoid sin. It is not easy to change jobs, remove friends from ones life or move, but it will be worth it.

> *And he said to all, "If anyone would come after me, let him deny himself and take up his cross daily and follow me."*
>
> Luke 9:23

Take up the Cross

The person puts to death the sin in their life and does not allow themselves to let it grow. At times, they may be ostracized as they follow the Lord and have chosen to pursue righteousness. The result is the right kind of thinking. Not allowing oneself to fantasize about sexual sin but keeping one's mind busy on the right things (Philippians 4:8). Some are confused when temptation does not go away. As long as we are in the world we will face temptation, but it will get better if we persevere.

But I say, walk by the Spirit, and you will not gratify the desires of the flesh. For the desires of the flesh are against the Spirit, and the desires of the Spirit are against the flesh, for these are opposed to each other, to keep you from doing the things you want to do. But if you are led by the Spirit, you are not under the law. Now the works of the flesh are evident: sexual immorality, impurity, sensuality . . .

GALATIANS 5:16-20

Feed the Spirit Not the Flesh
It comes down to a choice about whether one will feed the flesh or feed the Spirit. As one feeds the Spirit they become stronger. Though there may be times of temptation, as they continue to feed the Spirit these will decrease, though likely never go away completely. As one continues to follow the Lord there can be blessed results. One only needs to consider the life of "Rahab the prostitute." In the Bible, we are continually reminded of her past. This helps us see what can be as we watch what she becomes. She is in the genealogy of the Messiah, Jesus Christ. She appears to have married one of the leading men of Israel and to have built a family with him. They had a son named Boaz, who was quite the gentleman as recorded in the book of Ruth. One can have a much different life if they choose to consistently follow Christ.

Perhaps you are eager to go and help people who struggle with sexual sin, but you do not have access to them. Start where you are. Deal with those around you. Remember, this is a spiritual battle with high stakes.

> *For we do not wrestle against flesh and blood, but against the rulers, against the authorities, against the cosmic powers over this present darkness, against the spiritual forces of evil in the heavenly places.*
>
> Ephesians 6:12

This is the issue of our time, and we cannot afford to allow the mistakes of the past (e.g., Scopes) to be repeated. So get ready to reach out to, pray for, and minister to those entangled in sexual sin. If you are a leader, prepare those around you to minister in this changing sexual landscape. You cannot win this battle at the polls or in the courtroom. This is a different kind of battle that will not be won that way. It will be won through prayer, developing relationships, and sowing seeds of truth like Daniel so many years ago. It will be won one person at a time, by people whose names are largely unknown who have the courage to reach out to family, friends, and co-workers and help them out of this sexual trap. Let's embrace our mission to reach our world in this changing landscape. It will pay dividends by changed lives for all of eternity.

ENDNOTES

1. R. D. Putnam, and D. E. Campbell. *American Grace: How Religion Divides and Unites Us.* New York: Simon and Schuster (2010).

2. R. D. Putnam, and D. E. Campbell. Ibid. (2010).

3. J. D. Hunter. *To Change the World: The Irony, Tragedy, and Possibility of Christianity in the Late Modern World.* New York: Oxford University Press (2010).

4. *Taken from Center Church: Doing Balanced, Gospel-Centered Ministry in Your City by T. Keller Copyright © 2012. Used by permission of Zondervan. www.zondervan.com. All Rights Reserved.*

5. E. E. Moody, Jr. *Preparing Congregants to Survive, Thrive, and Influence a Post-Christian Culture.* Paper presented at the Theological Symposium. Nashville: Welch College (2014).

6. R. D. Putnam, and D. E. Campbell. Ibid. (2010).

7. D. Kinnaman, and G. Lyons. *UnChristian: What a New Generation Really Thinks about Christianity . . . and Why It Matters.* Grand Rapids: Baker (2007).

8. Pew Research Center (March 7, 2014). *Millennials in Adulthood: Detached from Institutions, Networked with Friends.* Accessed at http://www.pewsocialtrends.org/2014/03/07/millennials-in-adulthood/ on September 1, 2014.

9. D. Kinnaman, and G. Lyons. Ibid. (2007).

10. D. Kinnaman, and G. Lyons. Ibid. (2007).

11. D. Kinnaman, and G. Lyons. Ibid. (2007).

[12] *D. Kinnaman, and G. Lyons. Ibid. (2007).*

[13] *D. Kinnaman, and G. Lyons. Ibid. (2007).*

[14] *D. Kinnaman, and G. Lyons. Ibid. (2007).*

[15] J. Glass, and P. Levchak. Red states, blue states, and divorce: understanding the impact of conservative Protestantism on regional variation in divorce rates. *American Journal of Sociology, 119(4), (2014): 1002-1046.*

[16] *W. B. Wilcox. Soft Patriarchs, New Men: How Christianity Shapes Fathers and Husbands. Chicago: University of Chicago Press (2004).*

[17] *M. Regnerus. How different are the adult children of parents who have same-sex relationships? Findings from the New Family Structures Study. Social Science Research, 41, (2012): 752-770.*

[18] *D. Kinnaman, and G. Lyons. Ibid. (2007).*

[19] *D. Kinnaman, and G. Lyons. Ibid. (2007).*

[20] *D. Kinnaman, and G. Lyons. Ibid. (2007).*

[21] *E. Glicksman (December, 2012). Respect. Monitor on Psychology, 43(11), 32-35.*

[22] A. Novotney (March 2008). Preventing harassment at schools. *Monitor on Psychology, 39 (3) (2008):18.*

[23] *D. Kinnaman, and G. Lyons. Ibid. (2007).*

[24] *D. Kinnaman, and G. Lyons. Ibid. (2007).*

[25] *The Huffington Post (May 21, 2012).* Charles L. Worley, North Carolina Pastor: Put Gays And Lesbians In Electrified Pen To Kill Them Off. Accessed at *http://www.huffingtonpost.com/2012/05/21/north-carolina-pastor-gay-rant-starvation_n_1533463.html on September 1, 2014.*

[26] *A. C. Kinsey, W. B. Pomeroy, and C. Martin. Sexual Behavior in the Human Male: Volume 1. Philadelphia: W. B. Saunders Company (1948).*

A. C. Kinsey, W. B. Pomeroy, C. Martin P., and Gebhard. *Sexual Behavior in the Human Female: Volume 2*. Philadelphia: W. B. Saunders Company (1953).

[27] *D. Kinnaman, and G. Lyons. Ibid. (2007).*

[28] *L. G. McMinn. Sexual identity concerns for Christian young adults: Practical consideration for being a supportive presence and compassionate companion. Journal of Psychology and Christianity, 24 (4), (2005). 368-377.*

[29] Homosexuality Forum at Harding University: "What Should We Say to the Man on the Bus?" https://itunes.apple.com/us/podcast/what-should-we-say-to-man/id448945566?i=95484807&mt=2

[30] *D. Kinnaman, and G. Lyons. Ibid. (2007).*

[31] *D. Kinnaman, and G. Lyons. Ibid. (2007).*

[32] *R. Champagne Butterfield. My train wreck conversion. Christianity Today, 57(1) (2013):112.*

[33] *G. Robinson. God Believes in Love. New York: Random House (2012).*

[34] *R. A. Gangon. The Bible and Homosexual Practice: Texts and Hermeneutics. Nashville: Abingdon Press (2002).*

[35] *R. A. J. Gannon. Scriptural perspectives on homosexuality and sexual identity. Journal of Psychology and Christianity, 24(4), (2005):293-303.*

[36] *M. Regnerus. Ibid. (2012)*

[37] *A. Davidson (June 12, 2012). A faulty gay parenting study. The New Yorker. Accessed at http://www.newyorker.com/news/amy-davidson/a-faulty-gay-parenting-study on March 10, 2014.*

[38] *N. Frank (March 4, 2014). The Shamelessness of Professor Mark Regnerus. The Slate. Accessed at http://www.slate.com/blogs/outward/2014/03/04/mark_regnerus_testifies_in_michigan_same_sex_marriage_case_his_study_is.html on August 10, 2014.*

[39] M. Oppenheimer (October, 12, 2012). *Sociologists paper raises questions about the role of faith in scholarship.* The New York Times. Accessed at http://www.nytimes.com/2012/10/13/us/mark-regnerus-and-the-role-of-faith-in-academics.html?_r=0 on October 15, 2014.

[40] S. LeVay. *Gay, Straight, and the Reason Why: The Science of Sexual Orientation.* New York: Oxford Press (2010).

[41] N. Angier (August 30, 1991). *Zone of brain linked to men's sexual orientation.* The New York Times. Accessed at http://www.nytimes.com/1991/08/30/us/zone-of-brain-linked-to-men-s-sexual-orientation.html on September 13, 2014.

[42] American Psychological Association. (2005). *Answers to your questions about sexual orientation and homosexuality.* Accessed at http://www.apa.org/topics/lgbt/orientation.aspx on March 8, 2009.

[43] S. L. Jones, and M. Yarhouse. *A longitudinal study of attempted religiously mediated sexual orientation change.* Journal of Sex & Marital Therapy, 37 (2011):404-427.

[44] S. L. Jones, and M. A. Yarhouse. *Ex-gays? A longitudinal study of religiously mediated change in sexual orientation.* Downers Grove: InterVarsity Press (2007).

[45] R. L. Spitzer. *Can some gay men and lesbians change their sexual orientation? 200 participants reporting a change from homosexual to heterosexual orientation.* Archives of Sexual Behavior, 32 (5), (2003):403-417.

[46] B. Carey (May 18, 2012). *Psychiatry Giant Sorry for Backing Gay "Cure."* The New York Times. Accessed at http://www.nytimes.com/2012/05/19/health/dr-robert-l-spitzer-noted-psychiatrist-apologizes-for-study-on-gay-cure.html?_r=0 on July 10, 2014.

[47] S. L. Jones, and M. A. Yarhouse. *Ibid.* (2007).

[48] S. Gupta (October 4, 2011). *Study supporting gay conversion challenged.* The Chart. Accessed at http://thechart.blogs.cnn.com/2011/10/04/study-supporting-gay-conversion-challenged/ on July 12, 2014.

49 L. Hatterer. *Changing the Homosexual Male.* New York: McGraw-Hill (1970).

50 S. Jones. American Association of Christian Counselors (2002). *Homosexuality: What We Know from the Bible and Science.* Accessed at *https://itunes.apple.com/us/course/homosexuality-what-we-know/id547245977?i=118460781&mt=2* on June 10, 2014.

51 J. M. Bailey, and R. C. Pillard. A genetic study of male sexual orientation. *Archives of General Psychiatry, 48, (1991): 1081-1096.*

52 S. Jones and A. W. Kwee. Scientific research, homosexuality, and the church's moral debate: An update. *Journal of Psychology and Christianity, 24 (94), (2005):304-316.*

53 S. Jones. Ibid. (2002).

54 S. Jones. Ibid. (2002.

55 J. M. Bailey, M. P. Dunne, and N. G. Martin. Genetic and environmental influences on sexual orientation and its correlates in an Australian twin sample. *Journal of Personality and Social Psychology, 78 (3), (2000):524-536.*

56 G. M. Herek, A. T. Norton, T. J. Allen, and C. L. Sims. Demographic, Psychological, and Social Characteristics of Self-Identified Lesbian, Gay, and Bisexual Adults in a US Probability Sample. *Sexuality Research & Social Policy, 7 (3),* (2010):176–200. doi:10.1007/s13178-010-0017-y.

57 S. V. Vanauken. *A Severe Mercy (pp. 146-148).* New York: Harper One (1977).

58 R. E. Tanzi, and L. Bertram. Twenty years of the Alzheimer's Disease Amyloid Hypothesis: A genetic perspective. *Cell, 120 (4), (2005):545-555.*

A. C. Heath, K. K. Bucholz, P.A. F. Madden, S. H. Dinwiddie, W. S. Slutske, L. J. Bierut, D. J. Statham, M. P. Dunne, J. B. Whitfield, and N. G. Martin. Genetic and environmental contributions to alcohol dependence risk in a national twin sample:

Consistency of findings in men and women. Psychological Medicine, 27, (1997):1381-1396.

A. Caspi, K. Sugden, T. E. Moffitt, A. Taylor, I. Craig, H. Harrington, J. McClay, J. Mill, J. Martin, A. Braithwaite, and R. Poulton. *Influence of life stress on depression: Moderation by a Polymorphism in the 5-HTT Gene, Science, 301, (2003):386-389.*

[59] S. LeVay. *A difference in the hypothalamic structure between heterosexual and homosexual men. Science, 253, (1991):1034-1037.*

[60] S. L. Jones, and M. A. Yarhouse. *Homosexuality: The use of scientific research in the church's moral debate.* Downers Grove: Intervarsity Press (2000).

[61] W. Byne, S. Tobet, L. A. Mattiace, M. S. Lasco, E. Kemether, and M. A. Edgar et al. *The interstitial nuclei of the human anterior hypothalamus: An investigation of variation with sex, sexual orientation, and HIV status. Hormones and Behavior, 40, (2001):86-92.*

[62] S. Jones and A. W. Kwee. *Ibid.* (2005).

[63] J. A. Tabak, and V. Zayas. *The roles of featural and configural face processing in snap judgments of sexual orientation. PLOS One, (2012):DOI: 10.1371/journal.prone.0036671.*

[64] G. Wilson. *The Great Porn Experiment.* Accessed at https://www.youtube.com/watch?v=wSF82AwSDiU on June 1, 2014.

[65] D. Nimmons. *Sex and the Brain.* March 1994 Discover Magazine. Accessed at http://discovermagazine.com/1994/mar/sexandthebrain346 on April 1, 2015.

HELPFUL PODCASTS

Liberty University Convocation 2010: 2/12/2010. Alan Chambers, Leaving Homosexuality. He describes how he got into a homosexual lifestyle and through Christ left it behind. https://itunes.apple.com/us/podcast/2010.02.12-leaving-homosexuality/id427899317?i=92369476&mt=2

Secret Thoughts of an Unlikely Convert Rosaria Butterfield and Russell Moore
https://www.youtube.com/watch?v=cc8wPOHksYs

Homosexuality and the Church: Gordon Conwell Theological Seminary. A panel discussion on homosexuality. The last session is of a Christian who was saved out of the homosexual lifestyle. https://itunes.apple.com/us/podcast/lecture-1/id522683191?i=113974140&mt=2

ALSO AVAILABLE
from Edward Moody

An excellent resource to give to those who are struggling with sexual issues.

randallhouse.com
(800) 877-7030

d6family.com

DO YOU FEEL ALONE IN THIS BIG WORLD OF OURS?

Using Scripture and real life experiences, Eddie Moody shares powerful insight to help teens navigate the everyday challenges they face in society. With practical steps and resources, Moody moves teens to a place where they can thrive in their culture while having a real impact on the world around them.

Available at d6family.com

1-800-877-7030

DON'T LET FEAR HOLD YOU BACK.

MOVE BEYOND THE PAIN AND STEP OUT INTO **FREEDOM.**

The author shares details concerning the **emotional and physical symptoms** related to the subject as well as ways to overcome these difficulties.

Readers will find **words of comfort and hope** through Scripture, examples from the Bible of those dealing with difficulties, and practical advice on surviving the difficult situation they are facing.

A **list of resources** is given to encourage further help where needed.

ALSO AVAILABLE
from Dr. Moody

randall house
randallhouse.com
(800) 877-7030

d6family.com

D6 CONFERENCE

a family ministry conference connecting CHURCH and HOME through generational discipleship

D6conference.com

www.ingramcontent.com/pod-product-compliance
Lightning Source LLC
Chambersburg PA
CBHW031416040426
42444CB00005B/590